Original title:
Lost and Loved

Copyright © 2024 Swan Charm
All rights reserved.

Author: Liina Liblikas
ISBN HARDBACK: 978-9916-79-185-1
ISBN PAPERBACK: 978-9916-79-186-8
ISBN EBOOK: 978-9916-79-187-5

The Celestial Scar of Memory

In the quiet embrace of dawn's glow,
Cherished echoes whisper, soft as snow.
Each heartbeat a reminder, pure and bright,
Of the souls we've lost, now cloaked in light.

Time dances on the edge of grace,
Carving paths where shadows trace.
In the heavens, they softly reside,
Their love a beacon, our faithful guide.

The Sanctity of Tender Remembrance

With each fleeting tear, a prayer is born,
In the garden of hearts, where sorrow's worn.
We gather the moments, like sacred seeds,
Sowing hope where the spirit leads.

Memories linger, like stars above,
Each twinkle a testament of love.
In the sacred silence, we find our way,
Guided by light, through night to day.

Fragments of a Beloved Echo

Through the corridors of time, we roam,
In whispers of love, we've found our home.
Each fragment a story, woven tight,
In the tapestry of both day and night.

Voices resound in the stillness near,
A melody sweet, comforting, clear.
They sing of joy, of laughter too,
An echo of life, forever true.

In the Shadows of Reverent Silence

In the stillness where souls take flight,
We find our solace in the fading light.
The echoes of faith dance like the breeze,
In shadows that whisper beneath the trees.

Here lies the truth, profound and deep,
In the arms of silence, our spirits leap.
We honor the past, we cherish the now,
With hearts uplifted, we solemnly vow.

Unseen Grace in the Veil of Time

In shadows deep, where silence breathes,
The grace unfurls like whispering leaves.
Each moment laced with sacred thread,
In unseen realms, our spirits tread.

Through trials fierce, our faith stands tall,
A gentle touch in each heart's call.
The veil of time, a tender shroud,
Holds mysteries, both soft and loud.

Beneath the stars, our hopes align,
A dance of light, divine design.
With every dawn, a new embrace,
We find our peace in unseen grace.

The Silent Hymn of Longing

In the stillness of the night,
A silent hymn takes gentle flight.
Yearning hearts in quiet plea,
Seek the solace, wild and free.

Echoes linger, soft and bright,
Guiding dreams through endless night.
In whispered prayers, we find our song,
The melody of where we belong.

With every tear, a sacred vow,
Caressed by love, we breathe somehow.
Though miles apart, our souls entwine,
In longing's glow, the stars align.

Sacred Echoes of the Departed

In the hush of twilight's grace,
Sacred echoes fill the space.
Whispers soft from realms above,
Guide the weary with their love.

Stars alight, a guiding hand,
Hold our dreams in quiet stand.
In every sigh of the night air,
The departed linger, always near.

Through memories, they softly speak,
In every tear, their love we seek.
With hearts aglow, we honor them,
Their sacred light, our hidden gem.

Threads Woven in Divine Light

In every heart, a tapestry,
Threads of love and mystery.
Woven tight in radiant hue,
Divine light shines, ever true.

With every breath, a story spun,
In the dance of moon and sun.
Each thread a promise, pure and bright,
Guided by the hands of light.

Through trials faced, we find our way,
In tangled paths, we choose to stay.
Connected souls by fate's design,
In divine light, our hearts align.

Celestial Echoes of What Was

In the silence, stars reflect,
Whispers of love, soft and pure.
Echoes of faith in the night,
Guiding our souls to endure.

Mountains rise, shadows bow,
In the arms of the divine.
Time stands still, we remember,
Echoes of grace intertwine.

Hearts bound by threads of light,
Holding truth, sacred and vast.
Through the veil of memory,
We find the peace that will last.

Every sigh a gentle prayer,
Every tear a song unsung.
In celestial harmony,
Our spirits eternally young.

Together 'neath the vast sky,
We seek the light that remains.
Celestial echoes of what was,
In love, our heart still gains.

A Mosaic of Spirit and Remembrance

Each fragment tells a story,
Woven in the tapestry of time.
Life's colors blend in glory,
A mosaic, pure and sublime.

With every prayer we utter,
Windows to the soul unfold.
Threads of hope weave together,
In the warmth of love retold.

Gathered in a sacred space,
We honor those who once stood near.
Their laughter lingers in the air,
A symphony, both sweet and clear.

Memories, like scattered seeds,
Bloom in the garden of our minds.
Through the pain and joy of lives,
A mosaic of heart that binds.

In unity, we find our peace,
A circle blessed by grace above.
In remembrance, spirits dance,
Reflecting the power of love.

A Prayer for Those Who Wander

Lord of light, hear our plea,
Guide the lost on their way.
In shadows vast, let them see,
Your love's embrace through the day.

Through valleys deep and mountains high,
Keep their hearts safe in Your hold.
When they weary, lift their sigh,
Shower them with grace untold.

For every soul that drifts afar,
Let hope spark a flame anew.
A prayer for those under stars,
To find their way back to You.

In the silence of the night,
May they feel Your presence near.
With each step, restore their sight,
Wanderers, in faith, persevere.

In Your arms, may they dwell,
Finding solace in Your name.
With each journey, story to tell,
May they return, never the same.

The Hidden Sanctuary of Heart's Glow

Beneath the weight of worldly woes,
A sanctuary waits within.
Where love ignites and softly glows,
A refuge where peace can begin.

In the chambers of our hearts,
Whispers of truth often reside.
There, the spirit never parts,
A place where light and hope abide.

Through trials dark and roads unknown,
We seek the warmth of sacred grace.
In solitude, we're not alone,
The heart's glow, a cherished space.

In the stillness, prayers arise,
Calling forth the strength we need.
In its quiet, the spirit flies,
Unfolding dreams, planting seed.

Each moment a step toward light,
In the sanctuary of our soul.
Finding joy in love's pure sight,
A heart's glow, forever whole.

When Hearts Meet the Horizon

When dusk unfolds its tender grace,
Hearts converge in the wide embrace.
The sky ignites with hues so bright,
Revealing paths beyond the night.

Whispers travel on gentle breeze,
Promises echo 'neath ancient trees.
Every soul, a light divine,
Together, we are born to shine.

From mountain tops to ocean's floor,
In every heartbeat, we explore.
The horizon calls, a sacred song,
Inviting us, where we belong.

In harmony, our spirits soar,
Eternally seeking, forevermore.
Hand in hand, we journey forth,
United in love's endless worth.

As dawn emerges, softly it gleams,
Fulfilling the hope of our dreams.
In each moment, a truth we find,
When hearts meet, they're forever aligned.

Celestial Reverberations of the Past

Stars whisper secrets from afar,
Echoes of light, a guiding star.
In the night, they weave their tale,
Of crimson skies and silver sail.

Ancient wisdom in the air,
Every heartbeat, a silent prayer.
With each pulse, we sense the call,
In cosmic dance, we rise or fall.

Time as a river, flows and bends,
Carrying dreams where the journey ends.
Celestial notes in the silent deep,
Awakening slumbers, we're meant to keep.

In the stillness, we taste their grace,
Connecting threads in this sacred space.
Through the ages, our spirits find,
A sacred bond that leaves us blind.

Reverberations that softly sigh,
Reminding us, we'll never die.
In the tapestry of night, we see,
Celestial echoes, eternally free.

Shadows that Dance with Light

In the twilight's gentle shroud,
Shadows gather, playful and proud.
They waltz beneath the silver moon,
A duet of light, they hum a tune.

Every flicker, a story spun,
In the space where two worlds run.
Light and shadow, hand in hand,
Creating visions, graceful and grand.

As day departs, dreams take flight,
Shadows whisper secrets of the night.
In the contrast, a truth unfolds,
Through every heartbeat, life beholds.

The dance continues, forevermore,
In darkened corners, we explore.
With every step, together we weave,
The light of love, in shadows believe.

Awake the spirit, let it guide,
For in this dance, we shall abide.
Together, we find our sacred right,
In shadows that dance, we find the light.

The Pilgrimage of Sacred Longing

With every step, the heart draws near,
To sacred paths, we hold so dear.
The journey long, yet sweetly blessed,
In every moment, love confessed.

Through valleys low and mountains high,
With faith as wings, we dare to fly.
In sacred whispers, the soul aligns,
With every breath, the spirit shines.

Longing guides us, a tender flame,
In every trial, we seek the same.
Together as one, we climb the steep,
In the journey, promises we keep.

The road unwinds, a dance of grace,
In every face, we find our place.
As pilgrims, we walk hand in hand,
United in faith, we understand.

In sacred longing, the heart takes flight,
A journey endless, bathed in light.
For every soul, a purpose true,
In the pilgrimage, we find the view.

Threads of Light through the Veil

In shadows deep, His whispers call,
Threads of light break through the pall.
Hope unfurls like wings in flight,
Guided by the holy light.

Through the veil, the spirits soar,
Carrying grace from heaven's shore.
Hearts entwined in sacred dance,
Awakening faith in every glance.

Every tear, a prayer embraced,
In love's refuge, time is paced.
Unity in spirit's weave,
In each heartbeat, we believe.

With every step, the path aligns,
Faith ignites, the heart designs.
To tread on earth with purpose clear,
Threads of light dissolve the fear.

The Sacred Ashes of Yesterday

Beneath the stars of ancient night,
Lie the ashes of our plight.
In every ruin, wisdom grows,
From sacred fires, the spirit glows.

Yesterday's pain, a lesson learned,
In every heartbeat, passion burned.
From the ashes, hope is born,
In the dawn, we are reborn.

Life's tapestry, woven in grace,
In the silence, we find our place.
Every sacrifice, a stepping stone,
To the love that we have sown.

With every soul, the journey shared,
In reverence, our hearts have bared.
The sacred trust, a bond divine,
In the ashes, we intertwine.

In the Embrace of God's Silence

In stillness deep, where shadows meet,
God whispers soft, His love, a sheet.
In silence, hearts begin to see,
The sacred bond, you and me.

Beneath the weight of worldly noise,
In quietude, we find our joys.
Each moment spent in holy hush,
Brings forth a deep and sacred rush.

With opened hands, we seek the light,
In the embrace of endless night.
There lies a peace, profound and vast,
A broken past, lovingly cast.

In every breath, His spirit flows,
Guiding us where true love grows.
In His silence, we find our song,
In His embrace, we all belong.

Etched in the Tapestry of Time

Within the threads of fate we weave,
A tapestry of dreams we cleave.
Each moment counts, a sacred rhyme,
Etched in the tapestry of time.

Past and present, hand in hand,
In faith's embrace, together stand.
Life unfolds in colors bright,
In every shadow, is the light.

The loom of life with care we spin,
In the folds, the grace within.
Every stitch, a story told,
A legacy in love unfolds.

In every heart, God's purpose shines,
Guiding us through sacred signs.
Together we mend, together we climb,
Stronger still, in love's design.

Divine Murmurs of the Remembered

In whispers soft, the heavens call,
Echoes of love, they gently fall.
Memories wrapped in sacred light,
Guiding our souls through the endless night.

Upon the winds, a promise glows,
In every heart, a river flows.
Seeking the past where faith was born,
In shadows cast, our spirits worn.

A tapestry of hope we weave,
In every breath, the grace we cleave.
Awakening dreams, both near and far,
In silent prayers, we find our star.

With humble hearts, we rise and bow,
For in our truth, we stand in vow.
Cherishing whispers from above,
We walk the path of endless love.

Through Veils of Time and Tenderness

Time flows gently, a river bright,
Through veils of dreams, kissed by light.
Tender hearts hold stories dear,
In every glance, the past is near.

The hands of fate, they weave and twine,
Linking our souls, your heart in mine.
Together we stand, though seasons change,
In love's embrace, we feel no strange.

Through trials faced, our spirits grow,
In shared silence, the truths will show.
Every tear a lesson learned,
In faith's embrace, our spirits yearned.

As starlit skies witness our fate,
In unity, we celebrate.
A journey forged from joy and grief,
In every heartbeat, we find relief.

Sanctified Longing in the Heart's Sanctuary

In stillness found, the heart's refrain,
A sacred ache, divine and plain.
Yearning whispers in twilight's grace,
A longing deep for love's embrace.

Within the walls of sacred breath,
We seek redemption, dance with death.
Each unspoken prayer, a sacred plea,
Returning home, to set us free.

With every trial, our spirits soar,
Through sacred phases, and evermore.
In hidden corners, love ignites,
In shadows cast, it shines so bright.

Oft we wander, lost in night,
Yet in the silence, we find our light.
A journey paved by faith and grace,
In every heart, our holy place.

The Altar of What Was Lost

At the altar built of memories past,
We lay down burdens, free at last.
Every moment, a testament dear,
Hopes that linger, yet disappear.

In the quiet, echoes of love stay,
Whispers of dreams that fade away.
We light a candle for days gone by,
In every flicker, a heartfelt sigh.

The price of growth, the cost of pain,
But in the loss, our hearts remain.
Embracing shadows, we learn to heal,
In letting go, our spirits feel.

So gather 'round this sacred space,
In remembrance, we find our grace.
For every loss, a new dawn breaks,
In tender hearts, a love awakes.

Winds of Redemption in the Quiet

In the stillness, whispers call,
Beneath the sky, the shadows fall.
Grace descends with gentle sighs,
A chance for weary hearts to rise.

Through the silence, hope is sown,
Every seed in kindness grown.
Winds of change, they softly blow,
Leading souls where love can flow.

In the dark, a light so pure,
Faith and trust, a bond secure.
Let the spirit lift the veil,
As redemption weaves its tale.

Every tear, a river wide,
Flowing toward the seeking tide.
Hearts unite in sacred flight,
Sailing on through endless night.

Through the quiet, hear the sound,
Heaven's whispers all around.
In the winds, new life is found,
In quietude, our souls unbound.

The Choir of Fallen Petals

Petals drift on gentle breeze,
Each a prayer, a heart's unease.
Garden's grace in colors bright,
Whispers sing through day and night.

Gathered dreams in silence dwell,
In the fold of nature's swell.
Around the altar of our pain,
Beauty rises from the rain.

With every hue, a story told,
In soft embrace, the brave and bold.
Life's sweet sorrow finds its song,
Love's refrain where we belong.

In the twilight, shadows play,
Echoes of the light of day.
Fallen petals, spirits soar,
In the choir, we find much more.

Through the seasons, quietly,
Nature hums its symphony.
In every fallen, tender part,
Life continues, love's pure heart.

Notes on the Page of Memory

In the ledger of our days,
Every glance, a fleeting phase.
Pages worn from time's embrace,
Echoes linger, sacred space.

Each note penned in ink of grace,
Where the heart has left its trace.
Memories dance in candlelight,
Guiding souls through endless night.

Moments cherished, gilded past,
Hopes and dreams, forever cast.
In the silence, stories weave,
In the tapestry, we believe.

Soft regrets from journeys spent,
In the pages, love's lament.
Yet with wisdom, time redeems,
Life unfolds in radiant dreams.

Each memory, a thread divine,
In the heart, they intertwine.
On the page, the soul's intent,
Notes of life, our testament.

The Guardians of Heart's Remnants

In the temple of the soul,
Guardians stand, make us whole.
Through the trials, pains and strife,
Holding space for sacred life.

In the shadows, watchful eyes,
Steering hearts through weary skies.
With gentle hands, they heal the wound,
Anchoring spirit, love attuned.

Dancing flames of courage bright,
Kindred spirits in the night.
Every story etched in stone,
In their care, we are not alone.

Through the labyrinth of our fears,
They stand firm amidst our tears.
In their presence, truth unveils,
Guiding us through life's frail trails.

From the remnants, hope will rise,
Grace and faith, our greatest ties.
As we walk, hand in hand,
Guardians' love, forever stands.

Reverie in Sacred Landscapes

In sacred fields where lilies bloom,
The whispers of the Spirit loom.
Under skies so vast and bright,
We find our peace in holy light.

Winding paths through trees so tall,
In every shadow, we hear the call.
The breeze carries prayers softly said,
Each breath a thread, our spirit fed.

Mountains rise with ancient grace,
Nature's touch, a warm embrace.
In stillness, all doubts fade away,
In reverie, we choose to stay.

The streams flow with a gentle ease,
Each ripple, a song, a sacred tease.
With every footstep, we tread so slow,
In the landscape, our faith will grow.

With hearts aligned to heaven's tune,
We dance beneath the silver moon.
In harmony with life's sweet song,
We find a place where we belong.

The Chants of Hollow Echoes

In caverns deep where shadows play,
Echoes spring from hearts that pray.
Voices rise like incense sweet,
In hollow halls, our souls we meet.

With every chant, the silence breaks,
The melody of faith awakes.
Each whisper carries sacred fire,
To lift us higher, our souls aspire.

The walls respond with gentle grace,
Mirrored in love, we find our place.
Together we sing, though far apart,
In hollow echoes, we share one heart.

Through cave's embrace, the light descends,
A hymn of hope that never ends.
We sing in shadows, brave and bold,
In every note, a truth unfolds.

As we move through dark and light,
Spirit whispers, guiding our flight.
The chants weave a tapestry fine,
In hollow echoes, we intertwine.

Mosaic of Heartfelt Graces

Each piece a story, love's embrace,
In a mosaic of heartfelt grace.
The colors blend, both bright and dim,
Together in faith, we find our hymn.

Fragments shaped by pain and joy,
In crafting blessings, we find our buoy.
With every tile, our hopes combine,
In beauty's dance, our hearts align.

A tapestry woven with threads of prayer,
In every stitch, we show we care.
The edges rough, but love remains,
Through trials faced, our spirit gains.

As sunlight shines on varied hues,
In our mosaic, life renews.
Each moment captured, each heart entwined,
In this holy art, our souls defined.

With gratitude etched in every piece,
In heartfelt graces, we find our peace.
United we stand, in colors bright,
In a sacred bond, we find our light.

Beneath the Stars of Solitude

Beneath the stars, so vast and wide,
In quiet hours, we softly glide.
The universe whispers in the night,
In solitude, we feel the light.

Each twinkling star, a story told,
In the silence, our spirits unfold.
We reach for heavens far and near,
In every heartbeat, grace is clear.

The moonlight bathes the world in gold,
In isolation, our truths unfold.
With open hearts, we cast our gaze,
In sacred stillness, life's a maze.

Through solitude, we learn to see,
The beauty born from being free.
In every shadow, wisdom grows,
Beneath the stars, our spirit glows.

Connected still, though alone we stand,
In the cosmic dance, we take our hand.
Beneath the stars, we come to know,
In solitude, our hearts will flow.

Prayer Threads Woven in Time

In silence, we gather our thoughts,
Threads of faith spun from heart,
Each whisper a hope to the skies,
Woven gently, never to part.

Moments entwined in His light,
Guiding the lost back to truth,
Hands clasped in soft surrender,
Finding refuge in sacred youth.

Time's tapestry, rich and bold,
Each prayer a bright shining bead,
In the loom of the everlasting,
We find strength in every need.

Voices rise like soft morning dew,
Lifting burdens, lighting the way,
Chasing shadows with light unseen,
In the dawn of a brand new day.

Threads of love, stitched with care,
Connecting the weary and worn,
In this quilt of divine embrace,
We stand reborn, forever reborn.

Nimbus of Grief and Grace

A cloud hangs heavy with sorrow,
Yet grace drips like rain from above,
We gather our broken pieces,
Embracing both pain and love.

In the shadows where we wander,
Memories haunt like soft sighs,
Yet in the heart's tender silence,
The spirit finds ways to rise.

Nimbus wrapped in a warm glow,
Comfort in silence we seek,
In each tear that softly glistens,
Resilience grows in the weak.

Wings of angels surround us,
Carrying whispers of peace,
In the dance of grief and grace,
We find strength, we find release.

So let the storm rage above,
While peace dwells deep in our core,
For in this divine embrace,
We learn that love conquers more.

A Garden Where Angels Rest

In the garden, where silence dwells,
Soft petals brush past our hands,
Whispers of heaven, the fragrance tells,
A faith that forever expands.

Beneath the boughs of ancient trees,
Holy whispers are laid bare,
Each leaf a testament to peace,
In the embrace of love's care.

Barefoot in the sweet morning light,
We tread softly on sacred ground,
With every step, our spirits take flight,
In this haven, grace is found.

Angels linger like starlit dreams,
While shadows weave tales of the past,
With every prayer, our hearts beam,
In their presence, our sorrows are cast.

So come, weary souls, find your way,
In the garden where angels rest,
With every bloom, let hope sway,
In love's bosom, we are blessed.

Etched in the Divine's Embrace

In the fabric of time, we are drawn,
Etched deeply in grace's soft glow,
Each heartbeat a prayer, each dawn,
A reminder of love's endless flow.

In the tapestry woven with light,
Threads of hope shine through the dark,
With faith as our compass, we fight,
Guided by a gentle spark.

The canvas of life stretched wide,
Painted with tears and bold dreams,
In every shadow, He will guide,
Embracing us with sacred beams.

Every moment, a sacred dance,
In the rhythm of heartbeats we find,
Lost in the beauty of chance,
The love of the Divine intertwined.

So let us walk hand in hand,
Through valleys of doubt and despair,
For we are forever planned,
In the Divine's embrace, laid bare.

The Vessel of Remembered Light

In quiet whispers of the dawn,
A vessel holds the glimmers bright.
Each moment cherished is reborn,
To guide us through the sacred night.

With faith as anchor in the storm,
We gather strength from days ahead.
Our souls unite in sacred form,
As love's pure words are gently said.

The trials faced, like rivers flow,
Yet grace reveals a pathway clear.
With every breath, we come to know,
The light within will conquer fear.

And as we journey ever on,
This vessel carries hope so true.
With every dawn and every song,
We find our purpose, ever new.

So let us raise our hearts in tune,
To skies that hold a promise bright.
In every blessing, every rune,
We are the vessel of His light.

Grace Found in Forgotten Places

In corners where the shadows play,
We seek the grace that time forgot.
A gentle hand to light the way,
In every breath, a sacred thought.

The rusted gates, the overgrown,
Tell tales of love that once was there.
In silence, every heart has grown,
With whispers lost upon the air.

For every sorrow, hope resides,
In lonely paths and weary souls.
The quiet faith within abides,
As grace within us gently rolls.

In every leaf that sways and bends,
We find a beauty rarely seen.
From brokenness, sweet healing mends,
A tapestry of faith serene.

So let us wander where we find,
The echoes of a love divine.
In forgotten places intertwined,
The grace of God forever shines.

Sweet Sacrifice of Serene Absence

In stillness found where whispers dwell,
A sacrifice of love so pure.
In absence, hearts can hear the swell,
Of grace that beckons, sweet and sure.

For in the quiet, lessons grow,
Each tear that falls, a pearl of light.
In surrender, we learn to know,
The beauty found in blessed night.

Our souls entwined, though far apart,
In each reflection, love remains.
A bond that time cannot depart,
Through every joy and every pain.

As dawn breaks forth with colors bright,
We honor shadows of the past.
In every memory, sweet delight,
The sacrifice is never cast.

So let us find in absence, grace,
The lessons taught in quiet sighs.
In every heart, there's sacred space,
Where love transcends beneath the skies.

The Unseen Covenant of the Heart

Beneath the stars, a promise glows,
Invisible yet ever near.
In every beat, the heart bestows,
An unseen covenant sincere.

Through trials faced and battles fought,
A bond unbroken, strong and true.
In every lesson, love is taught,
To guide us on, to see us through.

With faith as light along the way,
We gather strength from every scar.
In moments frail, we learn to pray,
As hope ignites our guiding star.

Though eyes can't see what hearts embrace,
The whispers of the soul declare,
In unity, we find our place,
A love that lives beyond compare.

So let the hearts unite and sing,
A melody of trust and grace.
In every breath, the silence brings,
The unseen covenant we trace.

The Untold Stories of the Heart

In shadows where hopes blend and fade,
Yearnings dwell in the silence made.
Each heartbeat a prayer in the dark,
Carving paths where the spirits embark.

Lost tales weave through the weary night,
Guided by flickers of holy light.
Whispers echo in chambers of grace,
Unraveled truths in a sacred space.

Hands raised high to the infinite skies,
Seeking solace, where the spirit lies.
Within each tear sown in the soil,
Blooms the essence of love's sweet toil.

Voices murmur in the deep of soul,
Bearing witness to a greater whole.
In the untold stories, we find our way,
Embracing the dawn of a new day.

Faith dances in twilight's gentle sway,
Illuminating paths for those who stray.
With hearts open wide, in trust we stand,
Bound as one, hand in hand.

Vestiges of Grace in the Abyss

Beneath the layers of anguish and strife,
Lies the essence of a radiant life.
In the abyss, grace softly calls,
Breathing hope into shadowed walls.

Faint glimmers amidst the stormy night,
Whispers of mercy, a guiding light.
From the depths, the spirit ascends,
Finding strength where the darkness bends.

Each wound a vessel for love to flow,
In sorrow's embrace, our spirits grow.
Through trials faced in the fiercest gale,
The faithful heart shall never fail.

Hold fast to the vestiges of peace,
In the chaos, let your fears cease.
For within every sorrow, a seed of grace,
Awaits the soul's tender embrace.

In the silence, find the voice divine,
As love's embrace begins to align.
With every heartbeat, remember this truth,
Grace perseveres, restoring our youth.

In the Arms of Celestial Silence

In the hush of the night, worries dissolve,
In silent grace, the heart can evolve.
Swaddled in peace, the spirit takes flight,
Finding solace in the stillness of night.

Stars whisper secrets of ages past,
Guiding the seeker to moments vast.
In the arms of silence, be gently led,
To realms uncharted, where dreams are fed.

Beneath the heavens, where echoes cease,
Lies a quiet strength that grants release.
Each breath a hymn to the unseen light,
In celestial silence, we reunite.

Hearts entwined with the cosmic soul,
Infinite wisdom our spirits extol.
In the warmth of the quiet, let go of strife,
Embrace the whispers that nurture life.

In the sacred calm, we find our way,
In the stillness, love holds sway.
Every moment wrapped in divine embrace,
Awakens the heart, revealing its grace.

A Testament of Spirit's Whisper

In the stillness, a whisper is heard,
Crafting the dreams of the eternal word.
Every sigh a message, gentle and clear,
Testament of spirit, forever near.

Like rustling leaves in a moonlit dance,
Messages float in the night's expanse.
Listening closely to the heart's tune,
Unfolding mysteries beneath the moon.

In every struggle, a lesson obtained,
Spirit's whisper, forever unchained.
Beneath each burden, a truth resides,
Awakening life where love abides.

Threads of connection woven so tight,
Spanning the distance from darkness to light.
In spirit's embrace, our fears dissolve,
In whispered truths, our souls evolve.

Rise with the sun, let the heart take flight,
In each dawn's promise, find inner light.
For a testament lies in the echoes of grace,
In spirit's whisper, we find our place.

Canopy of Eternity

Under the stars, we gather close,
Whispers of love from spirits awake.
The sky unfolds a tapestry bright,
Binding our souls in the night.

Each heartbeat sings a sacred hymn,
In the presence of grace we stand.
Life's fleeting moments, a glimpse of forever,
Held gently in the Creator's hand.

Through trials faced and tears we shed,
Faith's gentle light leads us through dark.
In every shadow, a promise waits,
As we mark our path, a divine spark.

The canopy of time stretches wide,
Embracing us in love's deep fold.
We are but vessels of sacred truth,
Bearing the warmth of stories told.

In unity, our spirits rise,
Connecting us to realms unseen.
A dance beneath the endless sky,
In the canopy of eternity's sheen.

The Choir of Silent Heartstrings

In the hush of dusk, they softly hum,
Melodies born from hearts in prayer.
Each note a whisper, a sacred bond,
Resonating with love's pure air.

A symphony spun from silence deep,
Echoes of trust in the universe wide.
The choir sings of hopes unvoiced,
Wrapped in faith, forever our guide.

In every soul, a voice unique,
Together we rise, each spirit embraces.
A chorus for the weary, a balm for loss,
In harmony, our pain effaces.

With every tear, a note is born,
In the book of life, our lives are penned.
The choir holds us, their love surrounds,
In their song, we find our mend.

In silent prayer, we learn to listen,
The heartstrings strum a timeless tune.
In the quiet, faith blossoms wide,
Together we sing beneath the moon.

Emblems of What Was

In the garden of memory, shadows play,
Emblems of what was, painted in light.
Each petal a story of laughter and tears,
Time's gentle brush, both tender and bright.

We gather tokens of days long past,
Held close in our hearts, they softly stir.
Reflections of love, of paths we chose,
In every glance, their echoes endure.

Fragmented moments, like stars in the sky,
Sparkling brightly in darkness's fold.
We carry their warmth as we walk along,
With emblems of memories, precious as gold.

Even as seasons continue to change,
What was, remains in our spirits' flight.
The tapestry woven of joy and pain,
Guides us through shadows, toward the light.

In the embrace of the past, we find our way,
Each emblem a lesson, a shrine of grace.
For in what was, the seeds of tomorrow,
Blossom in hearts, in the sacred space.

The Celestial Weight of Longing

Beneath the heavens, we ponder deep,
The celestial weight of longing's fire.
In silence, our souls seek the unseen,
A dance of spirits, fueled by desire.

Each star a dream held close within,
A flicker of hope that never fades.
The universe listens, embracing each wish,
In the tapestry woven with love's cascade.

Whispers of grace flutter on the breeze,
As we reach for the light in the dark.
Yearning for peace, we navigate paths,
In the quest for truth, we leave our mark.

The weight of longing shapes our days,
In every heartbeat, a gentle call.
Through trials and joys, we find our place,
As stars align, we surrender our all.

In the embrace of the unknown we dwell,
The celestial pull, a guiding thread.
With hope as our lantern, we walk the night,
Carrying dreams where angels tread.

Revelations in the Quiet Heart

In stillness, whispers softly call,
Divine breath fills the empty hall.
From shadows deep, truth takes its flight,
Finding peace within the night.

Hearts attuned to sacred grace,
In silence, we behold His face.
Each moment holds a sacred thread,
Where light and dark both gently tread.

The quiet speaks, a hallowed song,
In solitude, we feel we belong.
Soft echoes of the ages past,
In stillness, love's shadows cast.

The heart unfurls like morning bloom,
In grace, it finds its rightful room.
Revelations come like softest sigh,
In the depths where the stillness lies.

Within the calm, the spirit's flight,
The quiet heart embraced by light.
In gentle trust, we rise and stand,
Divine blessings weave through our hands.

Divine Remnants of the Departed

In every tear, a memory thrives,
The light of love forever survives.
Whispers linger like distant stars,
In every heart, the echo spar.

Though bodies fade, their spirits dance,
In shadows cast, we find our chance.
To honor souls in sacred space,
Their essence lingers, love's embrace.

Through quiet nights and dawns anew,
The divine remnants softly grew.
In every prayer, a voice ascends,
Within our hearts, their journey bends.

We gather strength from those who've gone,
In silent hymns, we carry on.
The bonds of love do not dissolve,
In cherished thoughts, they find resolve.

Let us remember, let us hold,
The stories cherished, softly told.
In every heartbeat, life's refrain,
The divine echoes still remain.

The Sacred Embrace of Memory

In the garden where time stands still,
Memories bloom with a gentle thrill.
Each petal whispers a sacred name,
The heart remembers, never the same.

Through tender moments, shadows weave,
Memories linger in what we believe.
In sacred embrace, we find our peace,
Holding the past, love's sweet release.

In laughter shared and lessons learned,
The sacred fire within us burned.
With every loss, a gift bestowed,
In the depths of grief, our spirits flowed.

Each cherished thought, a guiding star,
Leading us home, no matter how far.
In the tapestry of those we've lost,
Their light remains, no matter the cost.

Memory holds us through the night,
In its arms, our hearts take flight.
The sacred weave of life and lore,
In every breath, love's richest core.

Light of Faith in Dusk's Embrace

As twilight falls, the world lies still,
The heart awakens with quiet thrill.
In dusk's embrace, we seek the truth,
A flame ignites, rekindling youth.

Stars emerge in the deepening shade,
Guiding us onward, never afraid.
Each flicker speaks of hope reborn,
In faith we stand, though weary and worn.

The sacred glow in night's caress,
Fills the void with ethereal dress.
In shadows deep, our spirits soar,
Finding grace on the sacred shore.

Though darkness may seek to cloud our path,
With light of faith, we can face wrath.
In the silent hour, courage blooms,
In every heart, prophetic tunes.

For in the dusk, our dreams take flight,
With faith as lantern, guiding light.
In love's embrace, we find our way,
Through every night, into the day.

The Essence of what Remains

In quiet grace, the spirit glows,
Embracing light, where true love flows.
Time whispers soft, on sacred ground,
In every heartbeat, hope is found.

Through trials faced, we rise anew,
In shadows cast, the light breaks through.
With faith as guide, the path we tread,
Unfolding dreams where angels spread.

The essence of what once has been,
A tapestry, woven in sin.
Yet mercy's touch, weaves joy from pain,
In every loss, a greater gain.

With open hearts, we seek the truth,
In every age, the spark of youth.
Life's fleeting dance, filled with grace,
In every loss, love takes its place.

In gratitude, we stand as one,
Beneath the stars, beneath the sun.
A melody of souls unite,
In harmony, we find our light.

Sacred Tributes to Unfading Joy

In praise we rise, our voices clear,
In every heart, the love draws near.
With hands uplifted, we celebrate,
The joy that lingers, never late.

Each moment shared, a sacred trust,
In faithful bonds, we find what's just.
The laughter shared, a gentle sound,
In unity, our joy is found.

Through trials faced, we stand as one,
In every storm, the strength begun.
With every breath, we seek to share,
The light of love, a timeless prayer.

With gratitude, our spirits soar,
In every heart, an open door.
Eternal joy, our guiding star,
In sacred space, we've come so far.

Together we build, a bright new morn,
In every soul, a hope reborn.
Sacred tributes, in song we raise,
To unfading joy, we sing our praise.

Cradle of Memories in Heavenly Haven

In quiet nights, the stars align,
Whispers of love, through ages shine.
In every tear, a memory flows,
In sacred hearts, the spirit knows.

The cradle rocks with gentle care,
In dreams we find, what we all share.
The laughter echoes, soft and near,
In every memory, we hold dear.

With open arms, the past embraces,
In the heart's quiet, sacred places.
Together we weave, a tapestry bright,
In heavenly haven, bathed in light.

Through trials faced and journeys long,
In every note, we find our song.
In love's embrace, we grow and thrive,
In memories, our souls arrive.

Cradle our dreams, in faith we stand,
United in hope, a guiding hand.
In heavenly haven, love will reign,
In every heart, joy's sweet refrain.

The Call of the Forgotten Heart

In shadows deep, a whisper calls,
To lonely souls within these walls.
A gentle tug, a prayer takes flight,
In darkness found, we seek the light.

With every beat, forgotten dreams,
Awake within, like rushing streams.
Hearts once silent, now break free,
In love's embrace, we learn to see.

The call resounds, through time and space,
In every soul, a sacred place.
The journey starts with every tear,
In searching hearts, we conquer fear.

With gentle hands, we heal the scars,
In every challenge, we find the stars.
The forgotten heart learns to sing,
In love's embrace, new life takes wing.

So heed the call, let spirits soar,
In every heart, we find the core.
Together we rise, with love impart,
In unity, the forgotten heart.

An Offering to the Forgotten

In silence they gather, shadows long,
Fading whispers of a sacred song.
Hearts once fervent, now lost in the night,
We offer our prayers, in humble light.

Time's gentle embrace has dimmed their flame,
Yet in our spirits, we chant their name.
With every tear, a memory unfolds,
A promise of peace that eternity holds.

To those unseen, whose stories we bear,
In the depths of our souls, their essence we share.
We light a candle, for their weary souls,
An offering made, to the ancient roles.

In the realm of shadows, their voices ring true,
Guiding the lost with a love ever new.
We stand in the gap, where the sacred resides,
In honor of all who the world now hides.

And as we remember, their spirits ascend,
A bond that transcends, where beginnings blend.
In this hallowed place, our hearts intertwine,
An offering made, to the Divine.

Fragrance of the Eternal

In gardens of wisdom, blossoms unfold,
Petals of stories, in silence retold.
The fragrance of truth, in the stillness we find,
Whispers of love that transcend space and time.

Beneath ancient arches, where shadows dance slow,
The scent of the sacred begins to bestow.
Each breath a communion, with souls ever near,
Awakening spirits, dispelling all fear.

Time like a river flows softly along,
Carrying echoes of the heart's gentle song.
In the stillness of night, the stars watch with grace,
As the fragrance of light fills this holy place.

With every moment, the divine we embrace,
In gratitude held, our hearts find their space.
A tapestry woven, with threads of our prayer,
The fragrance of love fills the still, quiet air.

So let us arise, and in stillness abide,
With the fragrance of the eternal as guide.
In unity gathered, we rise and we sing,
Celebrating the joy that our spirits bring.

The Sacred Bond Beyond Time

In the tapestry woven, our souls intertwine,
A sacred connection, transcending the line.
Through whispers of ages, our spirits converge,
A bond of the heart, in silence we urge.

Beyond fleeting moments, where shadows once played,
The light of the sacred cannot be swayed.
In the depth of our being, a truth we may find,
That love is a force that forever is kind.

As seasons do change, and days blend with night,
The bond that we cherish shines ever so bright.
In the stillness of prayer, we gather as one,
Embracing the warmth of the unfading sun.

From earth to the heavens, our hopes gently soar,
In the sacred embrace, we forever explore.
With each gentle breath, we honor our fate,
For this bond is eternal, a love that won't wait.

So let our hearts sing of the love that remains,
In the depths of our souls, through joy and through pains.
A sacred connection, a truth we hold tight,
Beyond time, beyond space, in divine love's light.

The Rapture of Emptiness

In the stillness we gather, where echoes reside,
The rapture of emptiness opens wide.
In the heart of the void, we find our true peace,
Releasing the burdens, our souls find release.

In shadows and whispers, the silence will grow,
Each breath that we take, allows us to know.
In the depths of our being, the emptiness sings,
A lullaby cradling the hope that it brings.

The dance of the spirit, in quiet delight,
Embracing the darkness, revealing the light.
In surrender, we find the strength to be free,
In rapture of nothing, we begin to see.

With every heartbeat, let go of the past,
Emptiness cradles, our fears are surpassed.
In the silent embrace of what cannot be known,
We cherish the stillness, our spirits have grown.

So let us be present, in moments so rare,
The rapture of emptiness beckons us there.
In the quiet of being, a wisdom profound,
In the depths of the void, our true selves are found.

A Prayer Adrift in Time

In the stillness of the night,
Whispers rise to the divine,
Hearts entwined in sacred light,
Lost in faith, yet we align.

Moments fleeting, like the breeze,
Time's gentle hand sways our souls,
Surrendered thoughts find their peace,
In love's embrace, we are whole.

Echoes of prayers softly roam,
Through the corridors of grace,
In this heart, we find our home,
United in a timeless space.

Tears of joy, like morning dew,
Fall upon the altar neat,
With each breath, we are renewed,
Guided by love's steady beat.

So here we stand, spirits bright,
Adrift in prayers, we believe,
Casting wishes into the night,
In the silence, we receive.

Angels Weep in the Quiet

In the echoes of the morn,
Softly an angel sighs,
With sorrow for the forlorn,
As tears touch the earth and rise.

Veils of sadness drape the skies,
In whispers of a gentle hope,
They carry our unspoken cries,
In their wings, we learn to cope.

Stars above begin to weep,
For the lost and the alone,
In their vigil, love runs deep,
Guiding spirits back to home.

Every prayer a soft embrace,
In the shadows of despair,
Angels weave a sacred lace,
Binding hearts with tender care.

Yet amidst the grief and pain,
A melody begins to rise,
Hope like sunshine after rain,
Reflects in celestial eyes.

The Altar of Silent Memories

Upon this altar, time stands still,
Echoes of laughter softly play,
In silent memories, love we fill,
As shadows dance in light's ballet.

Each token tells a sorrowed tale,
Of moments cherished, never lost,
In this sacred space, we unveil,
The beauty found in every cost.

Candles flicker, flickers of hope,
As prayers ascend to the skies,
In the stillness, we learn to cope,
With tear-stained cheeks and open eyes.

Here we gather, hearts entwined,
A woven tapestry of grace,
In silence, healing we will find,
As love restores each broken place.

So let the memories softly weave,
A fabric rich, from joy to pain,
At this altar, we believe,
In every loss, there's love's gain.

Threads of Affection Never Severed

Woven tightly, hearts align,
In the fabric of our days,
Threads of love, oh, so divine,
Together, we find our ways.

In the tapestry of time,
Every stitch holds stories near,
With each moment, life's a rhyme,
Joy and sorrow, one we share.

Though distance may stretch apart,
The bonds between us grow strong,
In the rhythm of each heart,
We find where we all belong.

With gentle whispers, love remains,
A melody that won't fade,
Through the trials and through the pains,
In every promise, we've made.

So let the threads of affection bind,
In unity, we shall rise,
In the depths of love, we find,
A tapestry that never dies.

Celestial Connections in the Quiet Dawn

In the hush of morning light,
Heaven's whisper draws us near.
Silent prayers take to flight,
In the dawn, our hearts hold dear.

The stars retreat, but still they shine,
Guiding souls through shadowed days.
Each heartbeat, a sacred sign,
In quiet hours, we find our ways.

Nature sings a gentle tune,
Echoes of benevolent grace.
Beneath the curve of waning moon,
We feel the warmth of a loving embrace.

Paths entwined by love divine,
As the sun breaks through the haze.
In every moment, souls align,
Connecting in celestial ways.

With every breath, we see the bond,
That links our hearts to distant skies.
In this sacred space, we respond,
To the truth that never dies.

The Peace of What Still Remains

In the stillness where time halts,
A whisper cradles weary hearts.
Amidst the chaos, calm exalts,
In every end, a new path starts.

The remnants of love softly glow,
A promise made in twilight's grace.
In memory's embrace, we know,
What once was here, will leave a trace.

Time may scatter, like autumn leaves,
Yet in the quiet, solace grows.
We gather hope, as nature weaves,
A tapestry that gently flows.

Each heartbeat echoes what we seek,
In every moment, truth remains.
The spirit whispers soft and meek,
Reminding us of love's refrains.

In shadows long, the light still gleams,
As faith abides through trials faced.
For in the quiet, peace redeems,
The heart's soft yearnings, held with grace.

Whispered Prayers of the Forsaken

In the dark, where shadows creep,
Voices rise, though hope seems lost.
Whispered prayers, our souls to keep,
In faith's embrace, we bear the cost.

Each tear a testament of strife,
Fingers clasped, our hearts entwined.
In the silence, we find new life,
As light breaks through the darkened mind.

Forsaken paths, yet still we tread,
Guided by love's unwavering call.
With every step, our spirits fed,
In unity, we rise and fall.

The broken, in grace, find their voice,
In harmony, they lift the loud.
From shattered dreams, we make a choice,
To stand as one, no fear allowed.

In whispered prayers, the heart is healed,
A symphony of hope in pain.
Through darkness, light is revealed,
Together, our spirits gain.

Echoes of Unseen Grace

In the grandeur of silent skies,
Where stars dance in their secret place.
We hear the truth that softly sighs,
Echoes of an unseen grace.

The world spins on, yet we remain,
Anchored by the love divine.
In quiet moments, we find gain,
A tapestry of hearts in line.

Beyond the veil, our spirits soar,
Touching realms we cannot see.
With every breath, we ask for more,
As whispers guide us to be free.

In gratitude, our hearts awake,
For every blessing gently placed.
In trials faced, we learn to take,
The lessons wrapped in love's embrace.

To walk in faith, to trust the grace,
That fills the void with radiant light.
In every soul, a sacred trace,
Of echoes that inspire our flight.

Whispers of the Absent Soul

In quiet moments, spirits speak,
Softly guiding, serene and meek.
Through whispered winds, their love remains,
A gentle touch, in heart's refrains.

Each tear we shed, a prayer in flight,
A bond unbroken, vivid light.
In our hearts, their essence stays,
Illuminate our darkest days.

In shadows cast, their voices rise,
Through sacred silence, sweet goodbyes.
Their laughter lingers in the air,
A testament of love and care.

As stars above, in night they gleam,
A promise held, a sacred dream.
In every sigh, a voice we find,
In whispered love, our souls entwined.

The absent soul, a guiding star,
With every beat, they're never far.
Within our hearts, their whispers dwell,
A cherished bond, a sacred spell.

Shadows of the Cherished Heart

In stillness deep, love's shadow lies,
A gentle breeze, a soft reprise.
Through moments shared, their essence glows,
In cherished hearts, true love bestows.

The laughter bright, the quiet tears,
A tapestry woven through the years.
Each memory held, a sacred core,
In whispered tales, we long for more.

Like morning light through fragile trees,
Their presence hums, like nature's breeze.
A dance of souls, through time we cling,
In every note, our hearts shall sing.

As shadows play upon the wall,
We hear their echoes in the hall.
In remembrance, our spirits soar,
Their love transcends, forevermore.

With tender grace, they guide our way,
In every dawn, in dusk's soft sway.
The cherished heart, a sacred place,
In love's embrace, we find our grace.

Echoes in the Divine Embrace

In sacred space, we find the light,
Echoes of love, in endless flight.
With each heartbeat, we feel them near,
Their silent strength, a whispered cheer.

In stillness wrapped, the soul can soar,
Through trials faced, we seek formore.
A bond of faith, so pure and true,
In divine arms, we're born anew.

With every prayer, we call their name,
In love's embrace, they fan the flame.
Each tear we shed, a testament,
To lives once lived, their love we spent.

In gentle night, their presence glows,
Through every path, our spirit knows.
A tapestry of hearts we weave,
By love's own grace, we learn to believe.

In sacred echoes, we dwell free,
With open hearts, we seek to see.
In divine embrace, we find our way,
In love eternal, come what may.

Faded Blessings of Dear Memories

In time's embrace, the blessings fade,
Yet in our hearts, their love is laid.
Each memory shines, a light so bright,
In shadows cast, we find our sight.

The laughter shared, the stories spun,
In faded tales, our hearts still run.
Through life's vast sea, their echoes call,
In gentle waves, we rise and fall.

With every dawn, we feel them near,
In whispered thoughts, they persevere.
Though years may pass, love's thread remains,
In faded blessings, peace sustains.

The tender moments, wrapped in grace,
In time's soft arms, we find our place.
Each loving glance, a legacy,
In memories dear, we're truly free.

Though faded now, their spirits soar,
In every heart, they live once more.
With gratitude, we honor each part,
In cherished memories, they fill our heart.

A Sanctuary of Silent Longing

In a quiet grove, shadows play,
Hearts whisper prayers, come what may.
Yet in this stillness, souls find rest,
Seeking solace, the spirit's quest.

With each breath drawn, the silence swells,
Echoing tales that the heart tells.
The stars above, like candles glow,
Guiding lost dreams where they must go.

Time drifts softly, like autumn leaves,
Carried by winds that the soul weaves.
In every sigh, in every tear,
A sanctuary built from hope and fear.

Hands together, we reach for grace,
Finding the mercy in this place.
A melody plays, tender and true,
In the sanctuary, old and new.

In the depth of night, a light shines bright,
Illuminating the path of right.
In silent longing, we rise above,
Connected forever, bound in love.

The Sacred Weight of Affection

Upon the altar, hearts laid bare,
Love's gentle touch, a sacred share.
Through trials faced, and joys bestowed,
Affection deepens on this road.

Hands entwined, souls intertwined,
In every glance, the light we find.
Eternal bond, no distance breaks,
In the sacred space, our spirit wakes.

Whispers of faith, in quiet tones,
Echo through walls of ancient stones.
The weight we carry, soft yet profound,
In love's embrace, true peace is found.

Beneath the stars, as shadows wane,
A promise spoken to ease the pain.
In fleeting moments, our spirits dance,
In sacred love, we've found our chance.

With every heartbeat, a prayer is sent,
In the sanctuary of love, we relent.
United in purpose, together we stand,
In the sacred weight of affection, hand in hand.

Divine Fragments of Forgotten Paths

In the twilight glow, old stories wait,
Fragments of faith that time can't negate.
Paths once walked in the dust of years,
Now echo with laughter, love, and tears.

Lost in the haze, the heart still knows,
Every turn taken, the wisdom grows.
In every stumble, a lesson gleaned,
In divine fragments, the soul is weaned.

Amidst the ruins, beauty unfolds,
In brokenness, the spirit holds.
With each step forward, we reclaim the past,
In the dance of life, shadows are cast.

The whispers of angels, soft and clear,
Guide the weary through doubt and fear.
In forgotten paths, the light will shine,
Illuminating the sacred design.

With courage anew, we forge ahead,
Embracing the love that never fled.
Through divine fragments, we find our way,
To the heart of truth, come what may.

The Radiance of Silent Blessings

In quiet moments, the spirit beams,
Radiating joy, like soft moonbeams.
Each breath a gift, each heartbeat pure,
In silent blessings, we find our cure.

The dawn awakens with gentle grace,
Painting the sky, a warm embrace.
With open hearts, we draw in light,
In the radiance, all wrongs feel right.

With every prayer, our voices blend,
In the sacred space where love transcends.
A tapestry woven with threads so bright,
In silent blessings, we take flight.

Through trials faced and mountains climbed,
We gather strength, our spirits primed.
Together we stand, hand in hand,
In the radiance, we make our stand.

In gratitude deep, our souls take wing,
Finding the freedom that love can bring.
In silent blessings, we resonate,
With the universe, love is our fate.

Divine Echo of Past Embraces

In whispers soft, the echoes dwell,
A love profound that none can quell.
In shadows cast by ancient light,
The spirit soars, embracing night.

With hands raised high, we seek the truth,
In sacred bonds of fading youth.
The past reveals its gentle grace,
Each memory a warm embrace.

Through trials faced, our hearts remain,
In faith we rise, through joy and pain.
The echoes sing of days long gone,
In the divine, we are reborn.

As twilight falls, the stars align,
Each glowing point, a tale divine.
We listen close, in silence found,
The past and present all abound.

O sacred moment, hold us near,
In every breathe, our hearts sincere.
Eternal love, forever blessed,
In divine echoes, we find rest.

Serene Solitude in the Light of Grace

In quietude, the heart does seek,
A whispered truth, so soft, so meek.
In gentle light, the shadows fade,
Serenity in grace displayed.

When chaos reigns, the soul must pause,
To find the peace in holy laws.
In solitude, we come alive,
To feel the grace, to truly thrive.

Each moment shared, a sacred thread,
In whispers soft, we are all led.
The light of grace, a guiding star,
In solitude, we know who we are.

Through trials faced and sorrows borne,
In quiet light, our hearts are worn.
Yet still we rise, in love's embrace,
In serene solitude, find grace.

O gentle heart, in peace abide,
With faith our doubts can surely hide.
In stillness, we are truly free,
In the light of grace, we see Thee.

The Testament of Time's Gentle Touch

Through sands of time, we weave and flow,
The tapestry of life we sow.
Each thread a tale, a lesson learned,
In time's embrace, our hearts are turned.

With every sigh, and every tear,
The testament of love draws near.
In gentle touch, we find our way,
As moments pass, we learn to sway.

The hands of time, with grace they mold,
In every story, wisdom told.
From youth to age, our paths unfold,
Each fleeting glance, a heart of gold.

Yet still we chase the fleeting days,
In memory's arms, we find our ways.
In time's embrace, we're never lost,
A testament to love's great cost.

O sacred clock, your toll we hear,
In beauty's grasp, we hold you dear.
The touch of time, a gentle guide,
In every heart, love must abide.

In the Guardian's Loving Memory

In shadows deep, a guardian stands,
With open heart and gentle hands.
A watchful eye on those they love,
In silence speaks the grace above.

The loving memories softly weave,
In every breath, in all we believe.
A legacy of warmth and light,
In guardian's gaze, our path is bright.

Through trials faced, we bear their name,
In every struggle, none the same.
For love transcends the bonds of time,
Eternal whispers, so sublime.

When nights are long, and hope feels lost,
We find their strength, whatever the cost.
In guardian's heart, we find our way,
A guiding star that will not sway.

O cherished soul, in peace you rest,
In loving memory, we are blessed.
Forever bound by love's sweet thread,
In guardian's embrace, we're gently led.

A Symphony of Memories in the Night

In the stillness of the Night,
Whispers of angels take flight,
Each moment a sacred tune,
Under the watchful moon.

Echoes of laughter resound,
In the shadows, love is found,
Every heartbeat a soft prayer,
Carried on wings of air.

Fragments of days long past,
In my soul, they are cast,
A melody sweet and clear,
Drawing the divine near.

Beneath the stars' gentle gaze,
We reflect on endless days,
Each memory a sacred song,
To our hearts, where they belong.

In the tapestry of grace,
Time leaves its soft embrace,
Faith ignites the darkest night,
In this Symphony of light.

The Candlelight of Enduring Affection

Flickering flames in the dark,
Illuminating every spark,
Love's whisper in the gloom,
A promise to always bloom.

Gentle light through weary eyes,
Revealing truth, where hope lies,
In the silence, bonds grow strong,
Candlelight sings our song.

Each flicker tells a tale,
Of journeys where hearts prevail,
In shadows, a warm embrace,
Guiding us through every space.

With each glow, a vow we make,
Through the trials, as we wake,
In the glow of love's delight,
We find strength, we find light.

Together through the darkest hour,
We bloom like a sacred flower,
Forever in this holy dance,
The candlelight of our romance.

Cherubs of Reminiscence Above

In the heavens, cherubs sing,
Sweetly soft on angel's wing,
Holding memories so dear,
A symphony, pure and clear.

Floating high with gentle grace,
They watch over time and space,
Each sigh a soft embrace,
Reminding us of love's trace.

With laughter in the breeze,
They brush away our unease,
In their golden, bright parade,
Every moment love has made.

In the stillness, hearts align,
Under the stars, divine,
Cherubs bring a loving balm,
In their presence, we find calm.

As they gather dreams anew,
In the sky's eternal blue,
Cherubs smile on souls below,
In their light, our spirits grow.

The Garden of Unseen Love

In the garden where dreams grow,
Unseen love begins to flow,
Petals soft, in colors bright,
Nurtured by the tender light.

Whispers of the wind unfold,
Stories of the hearts so bold,
In each bloom, a prayer is sown,
In this garden, we are known.

Among the leaves, secrets twine,
A tapestry so divine,
With every step, we draw near,
To the love that is sincere.

Nature's song, a sweet refrain,
Echoing through joy and pain,
As the blossoms gently sway,
Love's unseen hand will stay.

In this sacred plot we tend,
With hope and faith that never end,
The Garden of love will thrive,
Where the unseen hearts come alive.

The Remnant of Sacred Affection

In whispered prayers the faithful cry,
Each tear a testament, a sigh.
The embers glow of love divine,
A bond unbroken, rich as wine.

Amidst the trials, shadows creep,
His grace within the heart does seep.
With every heartbeat, sacred ties,
Eternal whispers, never dies.

The remnants left of what was pure,
In every moment, hearts endure.
Through storm and tempest, they shall stand,
Held together by His hand.

In solitude, the spirit soars,
To realms untouched, behind closed doors.
With faith as anchor, hope our guide,
The love of Christ will never hide.

And when the night seems long and cold,
The sacred stories yet unfold.
For in each heart, His light shall shine,
The remnant of affection, divine.

Celestial Sorrows of the Heart

In quiet corners of the soul,
Celestial sorrows, they take their toll.
The weight of loss, a heavy chain,
Yet in the grief, there lies the gain.

With heavy hearts, we seek the light,
Through veils of darkness, day turns night.
The stars above, they seem to weep,
For souls that wander, lost in deep.

Each tear we shed a sacred prayer,
A longing deep, beyond compare.
Though pain may linger, hope remains,
In every heartbeat, love sustains.

Through trials faced and burdens shared,
Celestial whispers, how they cared.
In depths of sorrow, we find the grace,
To see His love, in every place.

And when the dawn breaks through the haze,
We'll find His mercy, all our days.
Celestial sorrows, they lead us home,
In His embrace, we are not alone.

The Prayer for Those Beyond

In silent moments, souls we name,
For those who journey, free from shame.
A prayer ascends, our hearts entwine,
For love unbroken, pure, divine.

They dwell in realms of sacred peace,
Where sorrows fade, and troubles cease.
With every whisper, faith draws near,
The echoes sound, they still can hear.

O Lord, embrace them in Your care,
Let them feel Your presence there.
For every tear and every sigh,
Within Your arms, they'll learn to fly.

The prayer for those who walked away,
In light eternal, may they stay.
With love that binds us, never lost,
Together we rejoice, no cost.

And when our days on earth are done,
We'll meet again, two souls as one.
In faith we trust, no tale too long,
The prayer for them, our love stays strong.

In the Stillness of Sacred Absence

In the stillness of the night's embrace,
A sacred absence fills the space.
Yet in the quiet, voices flow,
With echoes of the love we know.

Each moment passed a grain of sand,
In time's vast ocean, we understand.
Though absence takes, it also gives,
In cherished memories, our spirit lives.

A heart once full now seeks to find,
The threads of grace that bind mankind.
With faith as shelter from the storm,
In every trial, His love keeps warm.

Through tears that fall like gentle rain,
We learn to dance within the pain.
For in the stillness, hope will reign,
The sacred love that shall remain.

And when the dawn unfolds anew,
In absence felt, we'll find what's true.
For in the soul, His light shines bright,
In sacred absence, there shines light.

The Canvas of Fleeting Days

Each dawn a brush, in light we wake,
A tapestry woven, choices we make.
Life's colors fade, yet beauty remains,
In every moment, love sustains.

Time's river flows, we drift along,
With every trial, we grow more strong.
The hues of hope paint skies of gray,
In fleeting days, we find our way.

Trust in the path that faith will trace,
In shadows cast, you'll find His grace.
Each heartbeat sings, a sacred sound,
In every soul, His love is found.

Embrace the change, let go of fears,
For in the storms, the truth appears.
In every tear, a lesson shines,
The canvas waits, where love aligns.

So cherish now, each fleeting hour,
For life's a garden, blessed with flower.
Through every season, the spirit stays,
In the canvas of fleeting days.

Embrace of the Celestial Void

In the night sky, where stars align,
A whisper of grace, divine design.
The vastness speaks, in silence profound,
In the celestial void, love is found.

Like grains of sand in the ocean's hand,
Infinite dreams in a promised land.
The universe sways, a celestial dance,
In the quiet stillness, we take a chance.

Within the dark, a guiding light,
The heart seeks truth, through faith's insight.
Embrace the void, where spirits soar,
In the unknown, we yearn for more.

The cosmic winds carry whispered prayers,
In the silence, He is always there.
The void cradles each fragile soul,
In His embrace, we feel whole.

So gaze upon the heavens high,
Let go of fears, let your spirit fly.
In the embrace of the celestial void,
Find peace, where love is never destroyed.

The Labyrinth of Heart's Remembrance

In the maze of life, memories weave,
A tapestry rich, we learn to believe.
Each twist and turn, echoes of grace,
In the labyrinth, we find His face.

The heart recalls, in whispers soft,
Lessons of love, that lift us aloft.
Through shadows deep, and light's embrace,
In every corner, faith finds its place.

Time will guide, where spirits roam,
In every heartbeat, we are home.
The past is written with strokes of gold,
In the labyrinth, His story's told.

So journey on, with courage bright,
Through winding paths, seek out the light.
In every echo, a truth unveils,
In the heart's remembrance, love prevails.

Embrace each step, let wisdom flow,
For in the journey, our souls shall grow.
The labyrinth awaits, with open arms,
In heart's remembrance, lies all its charms.

In the Shadows of the Divine

In the quiet dusk, when shadows play,
We find His presence, not far away.
In whispers soft, the spirits call,
In the shadows of the Divine, we fall.

Each trial faced, a lesson learned,
Through darkest nights, our hearts have yearned.
The shadows dance, with light intertwined,
A promise blooms, to seek and find.

In every struggle, we see His hand,
Guiding us gently, through this land.
Trust in the path, though veiled in night,
For in the shadow, there shines a light.

With faith as our compass, we rise anew,
In the shadows, there lies a view.
The heart finds peace in every sigh,
In the shadows of the Divine, we fly.

So walk with grace, through night's embrace,
In stillness find your sacred grace.
For shadows teach us what love can be,
In the Divine's light, we are free.

Prayers for Shadows in the Night

In the silence of the night, we pray,
For souls lost in shadows, who wander astray.
With whispers of hope, our spirits entwine,
Seeking the light, through darkness we shine.

O Lord, hear the cries, in this hour of need,
Guide us through shadows, in faith we will lead.
With love everlasting, a beacon we seek,
Strengthen the weary, uplift those who speak.

As stars twinkle bright, in the heavens above,
We call upon mercy, and endless love.
For every lost heart, may comfort arise,
Embracing the sorrow, we open our eyes.

In the shadows we linger, yet never alone,
For prayers become solace, in each whispered tone.
Through trials we journey, united we stand,
Trusting in hope, held tight in His hand.

So let us not falter, nor yield to our fears,
For grace guides the way, and love dries our tears.
Together we rise, hand in hand we ignite,
With prayers for the shadows, we follow the light.

The Light of What Once Was

In the glow of the past, we find our way,
Memories flicker, through night and through day.
The light of what was, shines bright in our hearts,
Guiding our footsteps, as life's journey starts.

We cherish the moments, both humble and grand,
Each blessing recorded, like grains of fine sand.
In whispers of time, the echoes resound,
A symphony woven in love all around.

Though seasons may change, and faces may fade,
The light of the Spirit, will never evade.
In laughter and tears, we find our own grace,
For God in His mercy, our hearts will embrace.

As flowers that bloom, in the warmth of the sun,
Each petal a promise, of battles we've won.
Reflecting on love, that supports and sustains,
In the light of what once was, true joy remains.

So hold to the memories, let them show the way,
For the light of the past, never fades away.
With faith as our lantern, we'll journey anew,
Illuminated paths, where hope will break through.

Cherished Moments Beyond the Horizon

In the distance we see, where dreams softly soar,
Moments cherished dearly, forever we adore.
With hearts full of longing, we reach for the sky,
Beyond every horizon, our spirits will fly.

Each whisper of dawn, a promise unfolds,
Stories of love, that the universe holds.
In laughter and kindness, we craft what we seek,
For cherished moments, are treasures unique.

As rivers run deep, and mountains stand tall,
Through trials and triumphs, we answer the call.
Beyond every shadow, in light we believe,
For life is a gift, and love we receive.

We gather the blessings, like stars in the night,
Illuminating pathways, with faith as our light.
In every embrace, our souls intertwine,
Cherished moments guide us, through love divine.

So let us rejoice, in the beauty we find,
For moments beyond, are forever entwined.
With hope as our anchor, we joyfully roam,
In cherished moments, we find our true home.

Beneath the Cross of Graceful Remembrance

Beneath the cross, in a sacred embrace,
We gather our hearts, and seek your grace.
In shadows we find, the light of your love,
A beacon of hope, from heaven above.

With every small prayer, we lift up our voice,
In moments of sorrow, we still can rejoice.
The weight of our burdens, at your feet we lay,
Finding strength in our kneeling, through night and through day.

In memories cherished, your presence is clear,
Guiding our way, through laughter and fear.
For beneath the cross, we are never alone,
In love's gentle arms, we have all that we've known.

With every heartbeat, our spirits unite,
In the warmth of your promise, draped in holy light.
We carry your message, to heal and to mend,
Beneath the cross, your love will transcend.

So let our lives echo, the truth of your grace,
In the stillness of night, we seek your embrace.
With faith everlasting, and hope shining through,
Beneath the cross of remembrance, our hearts are made new.

The Pilgrim's Solitude

In quiet moments, heartbeats pause,
A soul adrift with sacred cause.
Through golden fields and shadowed lanes,
The whispering winds call out my name.

With every step, the earth unfolds,
Ancient stories, softly told.
In solitude, a depth profound,
God's gentle presence all around.

Each tear a pearl, each sigh a prayer,
In the stillness, grace is rare.
Heaven's light breaks through the night,
Guiding me with love's pure sight.

The stars above, a thousand eyes,
Watching as the spirit flies.
In pilgrimage, I seek to find,
The sacred peace within the mind.

At journey's end, a promise waits,
For those who knock at heaven's gates.
In solitude, I've found my way,
To the dawn of a brighter day.

Illuminated Paths of the Beloved

Beneath the veil of twilight's glow,
Soft footsteps trace where love does flow.
Each path adorned in hues of grace,
A dance of souls in sweet embrace.

The stars above, a guiding light,
Leading hearts through endless night.
In every glance, the joy we share,
Illuminated paths, a holy prayer.

In every garden, blossoms bloom,
Echoing love that conquers gloom.
The flowers sing in colors bright,
Each petal whispers, "Hold me tight."

Through rivers wide and forests deep,
Promises made, and secrets keep.
With faith as our steadfast guide,
Together, love and hope reside.

As dawn ascends with amber rays,
We walk the light of sacred days.
With hearts ablaze, we journey on,
In paths illuminated—never gone.

Hallowed Whispers of the Past

In ancient woods where shadows dwell,
The echoes sing of tales to tell.
Each whispered breeze, a timeless sigh,
Connecting souls who dare to try.

Hallowed halls of memory fade,
Yet in the heart, the truth is laid.
Through trials faced and battles won,
The sacred thread spins stories spun.

The pages turn, the ink still warm,
In silence we find the sacred charm.
Where faith is forged through fire and rain,
In every loss, a holy gain.

With every footstep, voices rise,
In harmony, we hear the cries.
Ancestral wisdom, softly shared,
Guiding hands, forever cared.

As night gives way to dawn's embrace,
We honor those who shaped our space.
In every heart, their light shall last,
Within us dwell the hallowed past.

Soul-Stitches Across the Cosmos

In every star, a thread is spun,
Binding all that's lost and won.
Across the skies, our spirits reach,
In silent bonds, love's lessons teach.

The fabric of time, a grand design,
Woven with moments, divine incline.
Each heartbeat echoes, resounds in space,
A sacred touch, a warm embrace.

Through galaxies vast, we journey far,
Each soul a light, a guiding star.
Tethered by dreams that intertwine,
In cosmic dance, our fates align.

The universe sings in perfect tune,
A chorus bright, a mystic boon.
In every pulse, creation breathes,
With love's soft hand, the heart believes.

Together we tread, hand in hand,
On woven paths, the divine plan.
In the tapestry of life, we find,
Soul-stitches created by the mind.

Sorrow's Embrace in Celestial Hands

In darkest nights where shadows creep,
Sorrow's tears like rivers weep.
Yet in despair, a hand appears,
To hold our hearts and calm our fears.

With gentle grace, the light descends,
In tender whispers, love transcends.
Through the veil, a soft divine,
Embracing souls with sacred wine.

When burdens weigh and spirits tire,
Hope ignites a hidden fire.
Each pain will fade, each wound will mend,
In the embrace of love, our friend.

From sorrow's depths, we rise to sing,
With hymns of joy, our souls take wing.
In celestial hands, we find our way,
Transforming night into a brighter day.

So fear not, dear, in darkest hours,
For love's embrace reveals the flowers.
With every step, we find the grace,
Sorrow's embrace, a holy place.

The Lantern for Guiding Souls Home

Amidst the fog where paths are lost,
A lantern shines despite the cost.
Its glow a beacon through the night,
Guiding souls toward the light.

With every flicker, hope ignites,
Illuminating the darkest sights.
In silence deep, the whispers call,
Uniting hearts, embracing all.

The lantern's flame, a sacred trust,
A promise borne from ancient dust.
In every heart, a light we find,
To lead us home, forever kind.

As twilight fades and shadows blend,
The faithful light will never end.
Through trials fierce, we hold it near,
For in its glow, we shed our fear.

So lift your gaze and follow true,
The lantern's glow will guide us through.
Together we shall journey far,
With faith as bright as any star.

An Ode to the Eternal Connection

In whispers soft, we seek the thread,
That binds our souls, both living and dead.
With love's embrace, we intertwine,
In timeless dance, a sacred sign.

Through ages past, our spirits soar,
Connected deep, forevermore.
Beyond the veil, we hear the call,
A symphony of love for all.

In every heartbeat, every prayer,
The ties we share are always there.
With gratitude, we weave each part,
Eternal bonds within the heart.

So lift your voice, let praises ring,
For all the joy connection brings.
Through trials faced, in joy and pain,
Our souls united, love's refrain.

With gentle hands, we hold the light,
Guided by love's eternal sight.
In every moment, truth shall flow,
An ode to love that we all know.

Heartstrings in Sacred Symphony

In sacred halls where echoes play,
Heartstrings strum a soft ballet.
Each note a prayer, each chord a plea,
Uniting souls in harmony.

With tender grace, the music swells,
A timeless hymn that gently dwells.
Through every rise, through every fall,
The sacred symphony calls us all.

In melodies of hope we find,
The threads of peace that bind mankind.
Through every tear and every smile,
We dance together for a while.

Let rhythms guide the weary home,
In sacred spaces, we shall roam.
With open hearts, we give our thanks,
For love that fills our holy ranks.

So join the chorus, lift your voice,
In heart's embrace, let spirits rejoice.
Together, we will sing and sway,
In sacred symphony, come what may.

Beneath the Veil of Absence

In the silence of the void, we seek,
A whispering touch, a promise to keep.
Fingers brushing the edges of fate,
In longing's embrace, we await.

Veils of sorrow fall like night,
Yet hope's gentle glow remains bright.
Through shadows cast by the lost,
We find faith in love's true cost.

Each tear is a prayer released,
A heart's lament, the soul's feast.
In absence, we gather the meek,
Embrace the silence that speaks.

Beneath the stars, our spirits sway,
In the dance of night, we long to pray.
For in the depths, our souls do rise,
In absence, we find the wise.

So let the veil be lifted high,
As we journey beneath the sky.
For in the silence, spirits call,
In absence, we find the all.

Sacred Yearning in the Silence

In quietude where shadows lie,
Our hearts ascend to the endless sky.
In whispered prayer, we seek the Light,
In sacred yearning, we find our might.

The stillness breathes the words unsaid,
In every thrum, where spirits tread.
A melody of hope, pure and sweet,
In silence, our souls find their beat.

Yearning flows like a river's stream,
In the heart's embrace, we lose the dream.
Each breath a testament of grace,
In sacred silence, we find our place.

In the depths of night, we rise and fall,
Connected souls hear the Divine's call.
Every heartbeat a sacred song,
Together, we voyage, we belong.

So hold this silence as we pray,
In yearning's arms, we find the way.
For in our hearts, the truth resounds,
In sacred silence, love abounds.

The Heart's Pilgrimage Through Shadows

In the shadows where secrets dwell,
The heart embarks on a quest to tell.
With faith as the compass, love as the song,
Through darkness and doubt, we journey along.

Each step a beat, a rhythm divine,
In the clutches of night, our spirits align.
Through valleys deep and hills of strife,
The heart finds wisdom in the dance of life.

Past echoes of pain, through memories sweet,
In shadows, the sacred and the bittersweet.
With every trial, a lesson unfolds,
In the pilgrimage, our truth is told.

The dawn breaks gently, casting its glow,
Illuminating paths we daringly sow.
In every shadow lies a light,
Guiding the heart towards what is right.

Thus, we walk on this sacred route,
With courage and love, we choose to clout.
For every shadow serves a role,
In our heart's pilgrimage, we find the whole.

Chronicles of the Forgotten Soul

In the pages worn and time-stained,
Lie stories of hearts that love has gained.
Chronicles whispered through the night,
Of forgotten souls, longing for light.

Each tale a thread woven in grace,
Carved in the fabric of time and space.
In silence, we honor the past,
In memory's embrace, we hold steadfast.

Through trials endured and dreams deferred,
The essence of life's song is stirred.
For every soul, a purpose revealed,
In the chronicles, their truth is sealed.

So gather the stories of those unseen,
In the quiet corners, where love has been.
For in each silence, a tale unfolds,
Of forgotten souls, and their brave holds.

Thus, we become the keepers of lore,
In every heart's ache, we restore.
For in the chronicles, love's truth is whole,
In every word, the voice of the soul.

Beneath the Stars of Yesterday

Beneath the stars of yesterday,
We find the light from ages past.
In whispers soft, the night conveys,
The sacred tales, forever cast.

Each twinkle holds a prayer untold,
A longing heart, a spirit soared.
In cosmic dance, the light enfolds,
The dreams of those who once adored.

The heavens watch, our hopes entwined,
In each bright glow, a love remains.
We seek the truth that's redefined,
Beneath the skies in gentle rains.

The paths we walk, in silence tread,
The stories etched on earthly stone.
With every sigh, a world we've shed,
To seek the lands we call our own.

Awake, dear soul, to night's embrace,
The beauty found in every start.
For in the dark, we find our grace,
In every beat, a beating heart.

Reverent Memories in Ethereal Space

In reverent memories we dwell,
Among the stars, we pave our way.
Each echo whispers, 'All is well,'
In ethereal space where shadows play.

Time bends in light, a gentle kiss,
With every moment, grace descends.
We cherish all that we would miss,
As love's embrace, our spirit mends.

Oh, sacred void, you hold our tears,
A tapestry of joy and pain.
In quietude, we face our fears,
While seeking solace in the rain.

The stars align, their presence clear,
In whispers deep, our souls connect.
With every prayer, we draw you near,
In reverence pure, we stand erect.

So let us rise, our hearts awake,
Through trials faced, we shall endure.
For every step that we forsake,
In love's own light, we are secure.

Angel's Whisper of Forgotten Smiles

An angel's whisper floats on high,
Through realms unseen, where sorrows cease.
In gentle tones, they bid goodbye,
To paint our hearts with love and peace.

Forgotten smiles in twilight's glow,
Like morning dew, they softly gleam.
They guide our path, through joy and woe,
Each cherished glance, a sacred dream.

The echoes dance upon the breeze,
As memories weave their tender light.
We bow in grace, our hearts at ease,
Embraced by love, through endless night.

As darkness fades, our spirits rise,
With every tear, a story spun.
In angel's gaze, the truth implies,
That we are part of everyone.

So let us carry forth the flame,
Of love that binds us, soul to soul.
In every heart, a spark remains,
As whispers guide us toward our goal.

The Pilgrimage of Unseen Bonds

On pilgrimage, our hearts align,
In unseen bonds that time shall weave.
Through valleys deep, we seek the sign,
In every step, we dare believe.

The journey's long, yet filled with grace,
As shadows soften in the light.
Together we embrace each place,
Our spirits soar to newfound heights.

With every breath, a prayer ascends,
In sacred union, we are found.
The love we share, it knows no ends,
In tender words, our hearts resound.

Though trials rise, we face the storm,
With faith as our unfailing guide.
In bonds unseen, we feel the warm,
Embrace of love that will abide.

And when we reach the journey's close,
We'll come together in the dawn.
With whispered truth, the sun bestows,
New life awaits, forever drawn.

Milton Keynes UK
Ingram Content Group UK Ltd.
UKHW022119251124
451529UK00012B/601